A First-Start® Easy Reader

This easy reader contains only 59 different words, repeated often to help the young reader develop word recognition and interest in reading.

a	Grandma	mails	stamp
address	happy	next	takes
airport	have	office	thanks
bag	he	on	the
be	here	plane	then
big	I	post	to
birthday	in	puts	trip
cancels	is	reads	truck
carrier	it	safe	what's
city	Jimmy	says	will
code	Jimmy's	send	worker
comes	letter	she	writes
day	letters	soon	your
did	machine	sorts	ZIP
goes	mail	special	

The Special Letter

by Joanne Mattern
illustrated by Susan T. Hall

Printed in the United States of America.   ISBN 0-8167-4944-2

10 9 8 7 6 5 4 3 2 1

"Soon it will be a special day," says Grandma. "I will send a letter to Jimmy."

Grandma writes a special letter to Jimmy.

She puts a stamp here.

GRANDMA CAT
12 TIGER ROAD
KITTYVILLE, NJ
        07630

        JIMMY CAT
        464 CATNIP LANE
        TABBYTOWN, TX
              75204

She writes Jimmy's address here.

Grandma mails the special letter.

"Have a safe trip!" she says.

Here comes the mail carrier.

He puts the special letter in a bag.
He puts the bag in the truck.

The mail truck takes the special letter
to the post office.

What's next? A worker puts
the special letter in a bag.

Here comes a big truck! It takes the
letter to the big post office in the city.

What's next?

A worker in the big post office puts the special letter in a machine.

GRANDMA CAT
12 TIGER ROAD
KITTYVILLE, NJ
     07630

      JIMMY CAT
      464 CATNIP LANE
      TABBYTOWN, TX
         75204

The machine cancels the stamp.

What's next?

A machine
reads the ZIP code.

Then a worker puts the
special letter in a bag.

Next he puts the letters on a BIG truck.

The big truck goes to the airport.

Here comes a plane! A worker puts the special letter on the plane.

The plane goes to
a big city airport.

A truck takes the letter
to the city post office.

What's next?

A worker sorts the letters.

She puts the special letter in a bag.

A truck takes the special letter . . .

to Jimmy's post office.

Jimmy's carrier sorts the mail.

He puts the special letter
on the truck.

Soon the truck goes to Jimmy's address.

Here is Jimmy!

"Did Grandma send a special letter?" says Jimmy.

"Here it is," says the mail carrier.
"Thanks!" says Jimmy.

Happy birthday, Jimmy!
Here is a special
letter on your
special day!

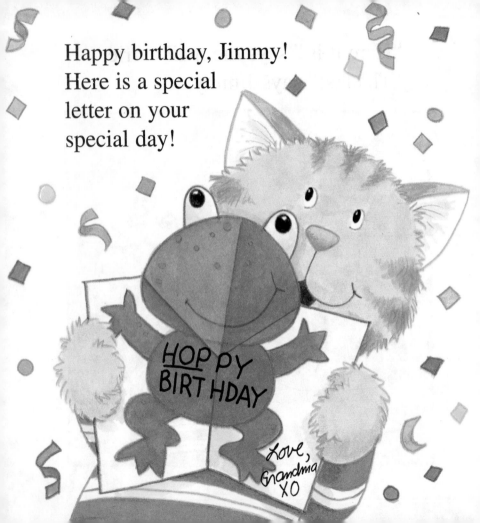